Shortcut

Earl Ayder
Illustrated by Cynthia McGrellis

Harcourt Achieve

Rigby • Saxon • Steck-Vaughn

www.HarcourtAchieve.com
1.800.531.5015

Level P

InStep Readers: *The Longest Shortcut*

Text by Earl Ayder
Illustrated by Cynthia McGrellis

ISBN 0-7578-9857-2

Rigby and Steck-Vaughn are trademarks of Harcourt Achieve Inc. registered
in the United States of America and/or other jurisdictions.

Printed in China

3 4 5 6 7 8 9 10 285 09 08

Contents

Chapter One

The Shortcut

"We could be swimming right now," said Mee, and her friends Diep and Khalid nodded. Their whole class had gone to Lake Eldon that morning for a camping trip. Mee and her friends had to stay behind to finish a science project. They were driving up to the lake tomorrow with Felix Romero and his father.

"We finished the project two hours ago, and now we have to sit here with nothing to do," Diep said sadly. At that moment, however, Felix rushed into the house. "Hey, everyone, my father doesn't have to go to work today after all," he shouted. "He'll take us to the lake right now, if you're ready to go!"

They all jumped to their feet joyfully and ran outside to Mr. Romero's van.

As they climbed into the van, Mr. Romero apologized for the piles of old newspapers in the back. "No problem, Dad," Felix said, as he settled into the passenger seat next to his father. "Our sleeping bags and supplies went on the bus this morning, so there's plenty of room."

The lake was only 150 miles away, but there were so many cars on the road that the main highway was a parking lot. The news announcer on the radio said that there had been an accident ahead. Although no one was hurt, police were still directing traffic slowly around the dented cars.

"With all of this traffic, it won't really matter that we left today," moaned Khalid.

"Yeah, by the time we get past that accident, it will be *tomorrow!*" Felix added.

Mr. Romero decided to leave the main highway. "I know a shortcut," he said. "There's an old dirt road that goes over Mount Wilson. I've taken that road a hundred times to get around traffic like this."

"Is that road safe?" Diep asked.

Mr. Romero assured her that the road was safe, and he started listing all his safety equipment—a cell phone, a CB radio, a first-aid kit, a flashlight, matches—until Diep felt better.

Khalid pointed to the bag on Diep's lap and asked, "What's in there?"

Diep opened the bag to show him what was inside: bottled water, snack bars, and a box of plastic trash bags. Khalid started laughing, but Diep said, "There are never enough trash bags when you're camping. I forgot to put this bag on the bus, but I'm bringing it now because we'll want snacks later."

Everyone, however, continued to tease Diep about her trash bags.

The air grew cooler as they drove up the road, and at last the heater had to be turned on. Then Mee pointed out the window and asked in wonder, "That white stuff on the ground isn't snow, is it?"

Mr. Romero said, "That's snow, all right. These last patches of snow may not melt for a while. It's warm in the valley, but up here it gets very cold at night."

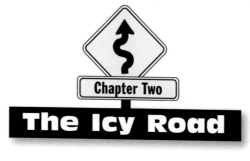

Chapter Two
The Icy Road

Suddenly, Felix yelled and pointed up to the hillside where a big boulder had come loose. It was rolling down toward them! Mr. Romero tried to stop the van, but the large rock hit the front tire and knocked the van toward the side of the road.

The road was icy and wet with snow, and the van slid sideways and over the edge of the road. A second later bushes and trees were rushing at them as the van slipped down the hill. Everyone screamed and anxiously looked out the window, searching for the bottom of the hill, but it was so far away that they couldn't see it.

The van slid down the hill about 100 feet when the wheels caught on some bushes and tree roots, and the van stopped with a loud crunch. Mr. Romero asked if anybody was hurt, and they all stretched their arms and moved their legs.

"We just have some scratches, Dad—it's a good thing we were all wearing seatbelts," said Felix.

"My arm feels bruised," said Mr. Romero. "I must have hit it on the steering wheel, but the rest of me is OK. I'll call for help." He dialed a number on his cell phone.

Diep watched as Mr. Romero's eyes began to widen, and she asked nervously, "What's wrong?"

"The cell phone doesn't work up here because the mountain is in the way," Mr. Romero replied. "I'll try my CB radio," he added, and he began to push the buttons on the radio. The radio didn't work either. Then he turned the car keys back and forth, but the engine didn't start. Mr. Romero said, "We have no power, and that means the radio and the heater won't work."

"But as soon as people know we're missing, they'll send someone to look for us, won't they?" Felix asked in a worried voice.

"Nobody will know we're missing," Diep said, her voice quiet with fear. "Everyone at the lake thinks we're coming tomorrow, and everyone at home thinks we're at the lake now!"

Chapter Three

Stuck on a Mountain

Khalid tried to climb past Mee so that he could get out of the van. "I'll climb up to the road and then run down to the main highway for help," he said.

Mee grabbed his arm and pulled him back into the van, yelling, "You can't run down a mountain road alone, just when it's getting dark. Besides, it's going to be very cold when the sun sets, and your clothes, like all of ours, are meant for summer weather."

"Are we supposed to just sit here then?" he asked in frustration.

"It won't be fun, but at least we'll be safe in here, and we won't freeze," said Mee.

Just then the van started to slide again, and everyone screamed. Though the car moved only a few inches downhill, everyone agreed that it wasn't safe to stay in the van.

"I guess I was wrong," Mee said to Khalid, letting out her breath. "We won't be safe in the van."

Mr. Romero warned everyone to get out of the car slowly in case it slid again. He waited for the others to get out safely. Then he kept his right arm pressed against his body as Khalid and Felix helped him out of the van.

Chapter Four

Staying Warm

"Dad," Felix said, "are you sure your arm is only bruised?"

"I studied first aid in school, and the bone in your arm may be fractured," Diep said.

"My teacher said to hold a cracked bone together by keeping it straight," said Mee. "We could use the newspapers in the van, but how will they stay on his arm?"

"How about these?" Felix asked, pointing to his long shoelaces. Mee rolled a newspaper around Mr. Romero's lower arm and Khalid tied Felix's shoelaces around it.

"Thanks. My arm feels better now, but that's not important," said Mr. Romero. "We have to stay warm until someone finds us."

"We'll need a fire and enough wood to keep it burning all night," said Mee. She looked at the sky and added, "We have to start gathering wood now because it will be dark very soon."

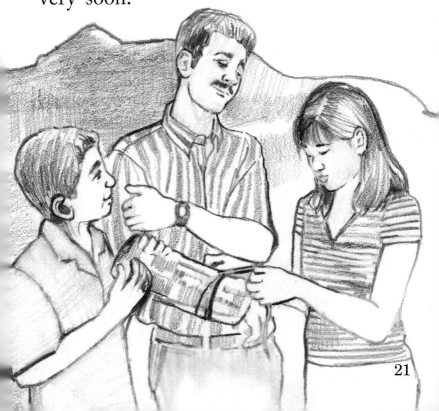

"All of the wood is covered with snow, and it's wet," Felix cried. "We need *dry* wood to start a fire."

"We should look for piles of branches," said Khalid. He explained that even if the wood at the top of a pile was wet, the branches underneath may be dry.

"We can carry the wood in my trash bags," Diep said.

"Stay together," Mr. Romero said as he sat down on a thick log. "Make sure to stay where I can see you."

They began to move across the hillside, searching for dry wood. They all thought that doing something— anything—felt better than doing nothing at all.

When Mee's trash bag was full of dry branches and twigs, she stopped for a moment and looked out over the mountain. She saw a tiny town beyond the woods and hills. She wished that they could somehow call to the people there or send them a message, but they were too far away.

Mee walked back to the group, pulling the plastic trash bag. The bag was heavy now because it was so full of wood. Her friends were crumpling up newspapers from the van and piling twigs on them, getting ready to start a fire.

Once the fire was burning, they all gathered around it and shared the snack bars Diep had brought in her bag. When those were gone, everyone was still hungry. Their stomachs growled as they talked sadly about the big dinner their classmates were probably having at the lake.

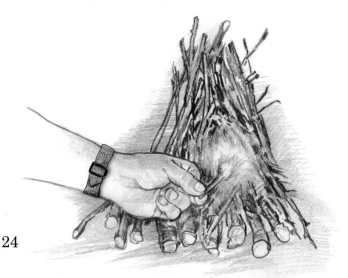

None of them had a coat, and therefore they were starting to shiver, even though they were sitting around a warm fire. They knew that it would get even colder as the night went on, and they were worried.

Chapter Five

Cold and Dark

"These newspapers feel tight," Mr. Romero said as he removed the newspapers from his arm.

"Oh!" Diep gasped when the light from the fire showed Mr. Romero's swollen arm.

"I read that ice helps reduce swelling," Mee said.

"There isn't an ice pack in the first-aid kit," Khalid said.

Diep grinned and grabbed a trash bag, and then she knelt down and scooped some snow into the bag. Khalid and Mee had retied the newspapers more loosely around Mr. Romero's arm. Next Diep gently wrapped the bag filled with snow around Mr. Romero's arm, making sure the newspapers stayed in place.

"This cold snow is helping," Mr. Romero sighed, but soon they noticed that his teeth were chattering.

Khalid said, "We have to help him stay warm."

"I don't know how we'll do that," Diep said, her arms wrapped around her body. "I'm shivering, and I don't even have a bag of snow on me."

The wind howled as it whipped through the trees, and they all huddled closer together.

Mee reluctantly said, "We might have to get back into the van."

Everyone stared at the van, but nobody moved.

Then Khalid said, "I think I have a better idea."

Khalid hurried to the van, opened the back door carefully, and came back with the rest of the newspapers. He crumpled up one page and gave it to Mr. Romero, saying, "Putting newspaper inside your clothes can help you stay warm."

"That's a good idea, but what I really need is something to stop this wind," Mr. Romero said.

Khalid took a plastic trash bag out of the box, and tore one hole in the top of the bag and one on each side. "Put this on like a T-shirt!" he said.

Mr. Romero slipped the trash bag over his head, put his head through the hole in the top, and stuck his arms through the sides.

When the others saw Mr. Romero, they started making trash bag coats for themselves.

They all looked funny wearing trash bags stuffed with newspapers, but they had stopped shivering. Then they sat around the fire, making conversation to stay awake. No one slept very well that night.

Chapter Six

Smoke Signals

By morning the group had burned most of their wood, but a few coals still glowed where the fire had been. Khalid used shreds of newspaper and some small twigs to build up the fire again.

The others saw Khalid working, and they stood up stiffly and started gathering wood to bring to him. Everyone was shivering, but they had gotten through the night, and now the sun was starting to warm them up.

After a few minutes, the fire was burning brightly again, and Mr. Romero told Khalid he had done a good job.

Then Mee walked up to the fire and threw a handful of wet, green leaves on the flames.

"Hey, wet leaves don't burn!" Khalid shouted.

"I'm trying to make smoke," Mee said, and she dropped another handful of leaves on the fire. Thick, black smoke started rising up from the fire.

Mee pointed west and said, "I saw a little town in that direction when I was gathering wood. If people in the town see smoke up here, they might think it's a forest fire and send someone up here to check it out."

They all gathered wet leaves, and the fire smoked heavily until Felix dumped a big bunch of dripping leaves on it.

"No!" cried Khalid, but his warning came too late, and the smoke died away. The fire was gone, and another one could not be lit, because they had used their last match.

They all stared sadly at the pile of burned leaves and twigs, barely noticing the buzzing sound in the sky above them. Moments later, a small airplane flew over their heads and went on behind the mountain.

"They were up too high and couldn't see us," said Diep unhappily. "We must look like ants to them."

Chapter Seven

A Big X

"The trash bags!" cried Felix, and the moment he spoke, everyone knew what to do.

Without another word, they grabbed the box of trash bags and ran to the biggest patch of snow on the hillside. They spread black trash bags on white snow in the shape of a big X, setting stones on the bags to stop the wind from blowing the bags away.

About five minutes later, the plane came back, but this time it flew around and around above the very excited group.

"They see the X, and they know we're here!" Felix laughed.

They were still waving and dancing thirty minutes later, when they saw the cars on the dirt road above them: they had been rescued.

Later, sitting by the ambulance, sipping hot cocoa, Mee told Diep, "We're sorry we laughed at you about those trash bags. They saved us!"

Diep shrugged her shoulders and said, "Everyone saved us, not just me. We all worked as a team!"

"That's true," Khalid agreed, "but without those trash bags, our shortcut would have been even longer!"